To the American Academy in Rome
M. B.

To Arthur Kremer, *primo magistro*
M. H.

Horace Satire 1.9
THE BOOR

Introduction
Latin Text with Commentary
Glossary of Terms
Bibliography
Full Vocabulary

For College and Advanced Placement Preparation

Margaret A. Brucia
Madeleine M. Henry

Bolchazy-Carducci Publishers, Inc.
Wauconda, Illinois

Editor
Laurie Haight Keenan

Contributing Editor
Gaby Huebner

Cover Design & Typography
Charlene M. Hernandez

Cover Illustration
Fragment of man (poet?) reading
From a photograph taken by M. A. Brucia

The Latin text of *Satire* 1.9 is reprinted from
Horace: Opera, ed. Edward C. Wickham and H. W. Garrod
(Oxford: Clarendon Press, 1963)
by permission of Oxford University Press

Horace Satire 1.9: The Boor

© Copyright 1998 Bolchazy-Carducci Publishers, Inc.
All rights reserved.

Bolchazy-Carducci Publishers, Inc.
1000 Brown Street, Unit 101
Wauconda, Illinois 60084 USA
http://www.bolchazy.com

Printed in the United States of America
2000
by United Graphics

ISBN 0-86516-413-4

```
     Library of Congress Cataloging-in-Publication Data

Horace.
    [Satirae. Liber 1. 9]
    Horace Satire 1.9 : the Boor / edited by Margaret A. Brucia,
Madeleine M. Henry.
        p.   cm.
    Introd., notes, and vocabulary in English; text in Latin.
    Includes bibliographical references.
    ISBN 0-86516-413-4 (alk. paper)
    1. Latin language--Readers.  2. Verse satire, Latin--Problems,
exercises, etc.    I. Brucia, Margaret A., 1948-   .  II. Henry,
Madeleine Mary, 1949-     .  III. Title.
PA2099.H67B78     1998
871'.01--dc21                                         98-29024
                                                          CIP
```

Contents

List of Illustrations vi

Preface vii

Introduction
    Horace: Life and Works ix
    Roman Satire xi
    The Boor: A Synopsis xv

Horace *Satire* 1.9: The Boor 1

Glossary of Terms 17

Bibliography 19

Vocabulary 23

Illustrations

Roman boys in school viii

View of Horace's Sabine farm x

Venosa by Edward Lear xiv

Apollo Musagetes xvi

Temple of Vesta 14

Statue of Horace 16

Inscription identifying Horace as the composer of the Carmen Saeculare 18

Preface

Horace is simple and complex, witty and serious, proud and humble. Perhaps he is all things at once nowhere better than in *Satire* 1.9. If a student were to read but one satire of Horace, 1.9, "The Boor," would be the one to choose. Its comic nuance gives life to the timeless and all-too-common situation of being trapped with an annoying and ill-mannered acquaintance.

Students reading *Satire* 1.9 will enjoy comparing and contrasting this lighthearted portion of "a day in the life" of Horace, a Roman of the Augustan age, with the more solemn addresses and meditations of his *Odes*. At the same time, *Satire* 1.9 provides the reader with a rare opportunity to take a short walk through downtown ancient Rome with Horace and his unwanted companion.

We are grateful for the help and encouragement we have received in preparing this book. We thank the Clarendon Press for its kind permission to reproduce the Oxford text; our colleagues at Iowa State University and Earl L. Vandermeulen High School for their interest in our project; our friends and colleagues on the Advanced Placement Latin Test Development Committee and at Educational Testing Service for the answers to many questions, large and small; and to the library staff at the American Academy in Rome for providing the perfect set of tools and surroundings for work.

There are, of course, a few special individuals whose help we want to acknowledge. Lou Bolchazy encouraged us to submit our proposal for publication. Barbara Dyer prepared the manuscript with great care and in the midst of numerous distractions. Laurie Haight was the most patient and thorough of editors. Bill Godfrey and his Horace class offered practical improvements. Liz Stephenson and John Breuker were enormously helpful in tracking down information about the Roman practice of *flagitatio*. Barbara Weiden Boyd made many thoughtful suggestions that greatly enhanced the clarity and coherence of the manuscript. And Nicholas Horsfall, a bibliography in human form, both directed us to a host of useful sources and saved us from a few errors. We are indebted to all.

We know that a careful reading of Horace brings instruction and delight; we hope that our *libellus* will help you attain both.

M. B. and M. H.

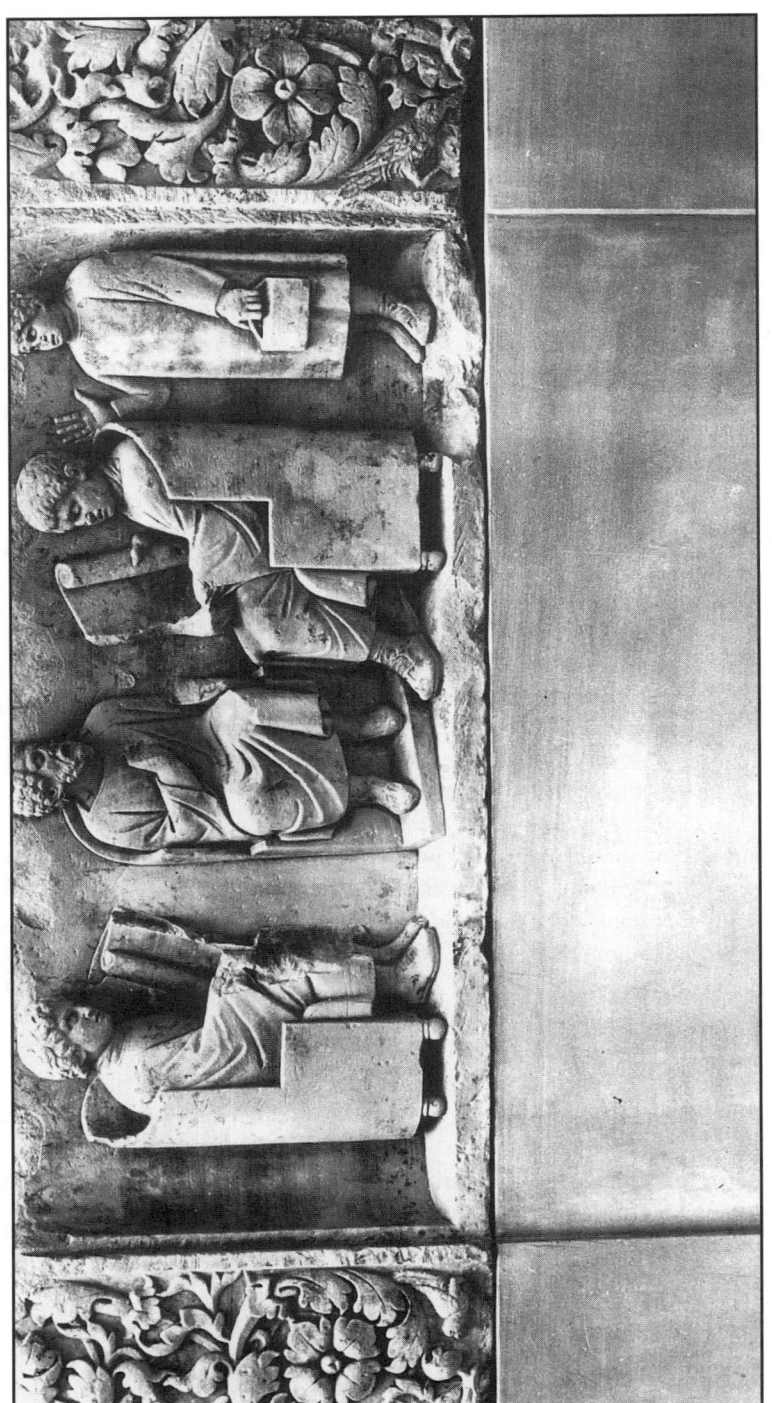

Roman boys in school. Courtesy Fototeca Unione, American Academy in Rome.

Introduction

Horace: Life and Works

As is the case for most ancient writers, we lack the kind of information about Horace's life that is available to the students of more recent authors such as Virginia Woolf or Mark Twain. Suetonius, who flourished more than a century after Horace's death, wrote a biography of Horace. Although his account has not survived intact and may have been derived entirely from Horace's own writings, some information can be gleaned from what is extant and from digests that were prefixed by ancient editors to collections of Horace's work. Horace himself drops many hints about his life in his own poetry. While the details can be debated endlessly, we can be reasonably sure of some aspects.

Quintus Horatius Flaccus was most probably born on December 8, 65 B.C.E. (His *cognomen*, Flaccus, means 'Flap-ear' and he does not explain how or why he acquired it.) His hometown was the Roman military colony of Venusia, located in southern Italy between Apulia and Lucania. Nowhere does he mention his mother; we can presume that he was an only child. His father was a freedman who, after moving from a small farm to Rome, worked in the auction business. Horace was educated in Rome by the *grammaticus* Orbilius, who did not spare the rod on his young charges. Our poet subsequently furthered his education at Athens in the mid-40s B.C.E.

This sojourn was interrupted by the political upheaval that followed the assassination of Julius Caesar in 44, and Horace enrolled in Brutus' army as a military tribune. If we can believe what he tells us in *Ode* 2.7, Horace was not a loyal soldier and deserted his troops in the clash between the army of Brutus and the combined forces of Octavius and Mark Antony at Philippi in 42 B.C.E. He subsequently suffered the confiscation of his family's farm after the defeat of the armies of the assassins. In 41, an amnesty enabled Horace to return to Rome. There he became a *scriba quaestorius* or senior civil servant, sometimes described as a clerk. This was a good position, which suggests some rise in Horace's fortunes or perhaps an ability to succeed within the system. Just a few years later, in 38, he was presented by his friends Varius and Vergil to the wealthy patron Maecenas, who was also a minister to Octavian. That association proved fruitful for Horace and enabled him to have the wherewithal needed to write his great works: in around 33 Maecenas gave Horace a farm, a perfect writer's retreat, in the Sabine woods.

Horace seems never to have left Italy after this time, though he frequented Baiae, the coast west of Naples, and Tarentum. He published books of satires (called *sermones*), epodes, odes, and epistles, as well as a poem written to commemorate Augustus' patriotic celebration of Rome's new age of peace and prosperity. The first book of satires appeared between 35 and 33. The second book of satires came out together with the epodes in 30, although the epodes were probably written between 41 and 30. The odes, collected into three books, were published in 23, but were probably begun around 30. In 20 B.C.E., Horace published the first book of epistles. His next production, in 17 B.C.E., was the *Carmen Saeculare*, a prayer to Apollo and Diana, asking them to bless Augustus' government. In or after 13 B.C.E., Horace published a fourth book of odes. The second book of epistles may have been published posthumously, and was written between 19 and 13 B.C.E.

We know nothing about the last five years of Horace's life, but he is said by Suetonius to have died at the age of fifty-seven on November 27, 8 B.C.E. He was reputedly buried on the Esquiline hill near his close friend and patron Maecenas. Suetonius' anecdotes and Horace's own *Epistle* 2.1 give us the portrait of a short, plump libertine who was beloved of Augustus and called by him a *homuncio lepidissimus* (most charming little fellow).

Whatever the truth of these impressions—which may have been cultivated by the poet himself—Horace's poetry demonstrates powerful erudition, a mastery of poetic discipline and technique, and a philosophic depth that, despite its fluidity, no mere dilettante could have dashed off casually.

View of Horace's Sabine farm. Photo by M. A. Brucia.

Roman Satire

The etymology of *satura*, the Latin word for "satire," is as unclear as the literary form it describes. It probably derives from the Latin root *sat-* meaning "full" or "varied" which gives us words like *satis* (enough) and *satur* (mixture). Diomedes, a late fourth- or early fifth-century grammarian, has offered a few possibilities, including derivation from the words *lanx satura*, a plate filled with a variety of agricultural products and offered to the gods; or from *satura* meaning a stuffing comprised of grapes, barley, pine nuts, honey, and pomegranates; or from *lex satura*, a law that incorporated many different items in one proposal. All these explanations share the concept of an abundant mixture, or of a variety. Surely inherent in the supposed explanation of the term is the acknowledgment that collections of satire were varied, presumably in subject matter.

• Satire Before Horace

Ennius (239–169 B.C.E.) first applied the term *satura* to writing. He composed four books of satires, of which a scant thirty-three lines or partial lines, quoted by later authors, survive. Though there was probably a Greek source for each of Ennius' satires, there appears to have been no parallel grouping of works in Greek literature. The surviving fragments of Ennius were written in trochaic lines of seven feet (trochaic septenarii) and employed dialogue. We know the subject matter of two of his satires—an argument between personifications of life and death, and a story about a mother lark who evacuates her chicks from a field about to be harvested by a farmer and his son. It appears that Ennius' collection of satires, in keeping with the meaning of the root word, was a miscellany. Criticism, which has become the staple feature of satire, was for Ennius just one of a variety of moods expressed in his poetry. Ennius may rightly be dubbed the father of satire, but those who followed him further shaped and defined the genre.

Though others had a hand in the writing of satire, four Latin authors are luminaries in the field: Lucilius (180–102/1 B.C.E.); Horace (65–8 B.C.E.); Persius (C.E. 34–62); and Juvenal (first century C.E.). Probably thanks to Juvenal's acid pen, satire is now most commonly assessed by how much it "bites."

Lucilius was an extrovert whose learnedness, openness, incisiveness, and great wit were praised by Quintilian (10.1.94) and whom Horace lauded as the discoverer of the genre. He composed thirty books of satires, now almost completely lost. These provide themes that became famous among subsequent writers of satire. Horace flattered Lucilius by imitation in his own *Satire* 1.4, but accused him of being rough (*durus componere versus*), too hasty in composition (*in hora saepe ducentos, ut magnum, versus dictabat stans pede in uno*), and not careful enough (*piger scribendi ferre laborem*). Indeed, Lucilius, "while developing the element of variety and role of the poet, gave it [satire] a clearer identity by focusing on the critical element and molding the dactylic hexameter to serve as the vehicle of expression" (Ramage 52). Because he was a man of the Republic and an *eques*, Lucilius enjoyed great freedom of speech and variety in the subjects of his criticism.

• Horace

Horace aimed for an exposition more elegant than that of Lucilius. The influence exerted on Horace by Catullus and his circle of "new poets" (*novi poetae*) on shaping poetic taste was profound. This group, known as neoterics, loved trendy language; Catullus' own openness both to writing about subjects drawn from the realities of daily life and to sharing his inner thoughts were to leave their mark on Horace's satiric poetry. *Satire* 1.9, in particular, with its flip, colloquial speech, clever repartee, and emphasis on the poet's personal and internal response to an increasingly uncomfortable situation, reflect those Catullan influences. In fact, this satire invites comparison with Catullus 10. Both poems take place in the Forum, both involve a chance meeting and conversation with another, and in both the poet tries to extricate himself from an awkward and uncomfortable social situation.

Horace's style in the satires is relatively easy to read and is not undeserving of the descriptive phrase *sermo cotidianus*, "everyday conversation." Initially he referred to his satires as *sermones* or "talks," e.g. at *Satire* 1.4, 42–48, and it was not until the publication of his second book, five years after the first, that he employed the word *satura* to designate both the genre of satire and the individual poems. Though Horace may appear, by our standards, to have been reluctant to use the word *satura*, Roman authors did not commonly employ generic literary terms to describe their writing. The absence of the term does not mean that Horace considered Book 1 something other than satire.

The writings of Horace fall into two groups—odes and epodes, and satires and epistles. Just as the odes are an outgrowth and development of his earlier epodes, so the epistles mark a return to the subject matter and, in a sense, are an outgrowth of the satires. Whereas the satires offer little other than criticism (i.e., there are no real suggestions for improving situations), the epistles are a philosophical extension of the satires. Written in informal hexameters, they maintain the stylistic ease and flow of the satires, but are considerably more positive in tone.

• Satire after Horace

Persius, infused with Stoicism and writing at a time marked by considerably less literary freedom, kept a comfortable philosophical distance between himself and his targets. Although Persius' stylistic debt to Horace is great, restraint pervades his work. In his short life, which ended at the age of twenty-eight, he wrote only six satires (as an ancient biography states, *scriptitavit et raro et tarde*, "he was in the habit of writing infrequently and slowly"). These criticized the frivolity of contemporary poetry, vanity, religious hypocrisy, sloth, enslavement to the passions, and avarice.

Juvenal wrote in a brief window of restored freedom of expression after the conclusion of Domitian's oppressive rule. In his sixteen satires, Juvenal unabashedly expressed his anger and outrage at human folly and excess in a political climate that finally made permissible this airing of grievances. As he says, *difficile est saturam non scribere*, "it is difficult not to write satire" (1.30). Juvenal also notes that it is easier to aim at targets that are dead. Though he was practically unknown for 250 years after his death, Juvenal was rediscovered with a flourish and "proved that satire need not take second place in the hierarchy of literary forms" (Ramage 168). In his works are found indignation, vicious invective, Stoic detachment, and resignation. Two of his most famous satires are the sixth, which castigates women, and the tenth, sometimes called "On the Vanity of Human Wishes." Of interest to readers of Horace's *Satire* 1.9 is Juvenal's third satire, a critique of the city of Rome.

Although Lucilius, Horace, Persius, and Juvenal all had vastly different styles and each was the product of his own times, nevertheless, each writer contributed to shaping the genre. Roman satire can be characterized by certain unifying elements: the presence of a recognizable poetic personality; variety of subject matter; informal meter; and the essential presence of criticism (see Ramage, et al., 2). Because social criticism became a hallmark of Roman satire, the political climate and degree to which freedom of expression was allowed imposed varying constraints upon the author.

Highly characteristic of Roman satire is the presence of the *persona* or "mask" of the author. It is not always easy to distinguish between the poetic "I" of literature and what might have been the actual beliefs or experiences of the author. When Horace's poetic "I" (or *persona*) says, "I happened to be walking along the via Sacra" we are not to conclude that Horace has had an experience just like that described in the poem. Because a theme, topic, or topos might become a standard ingredient of the genre—for example to criticize those who overeat—it does not necessarily follow that Horace, Persius, or Juvenal personally disliked those who overate. By studying the origin and development of Roman satire, we can better understand what factors influenced Horace and how he reacted to them. Similarly, we can see how Horace contributed to the subsequent development of Roman satire.

Photo: *Venosa* by Edward Lear. The Toledo Museum of Art; purchased with funds from the Libbey Endowment, gift of Edward Drummond Libbey.

The Boor

Satire 1.9, written between 38 and 35 B.C.E., is perhaps the best loved and most familiar of all of Horace's satires. Its universal appeal stems from the fact that the situation is one so pure, simple, and common that anyone can relate to it. For who has not been pestered by a favor-seeker transparently disguised as a friend? By endearingly making himself the victim and drawing the reader into his predicament, Horace solicits our sympathy and heightens the poem's appeal.

The action takes place almost entirely through dialogue and the satire exhibits many other features associated with drama, specifically comedy. It is traditional when discussing Roman satire to identify the poet/speaker as the *persona*, which means "mask"; and therefore this dramatic element of satire is acknowledged. The piece observes the unities of time and place; it can be divided into four "acts" (1–21, 21–43, 43–74, 74–78); sight gags and asides abound; the language is quick-paced and colloquial; and the story is resolved by coincidence and divine intervention, a *deus ex machina*.

In "Act 1" (lines 1–21) Horace has set out for a morning stroll in the center of town. A person he barely knows accosts him. Horace is polite, but dismissive; he would rather be alone. The Boor ignores (or is oblivious to) the hint and tries to impress Horace with his literary and artistic accomplishments. Horace is too polite to be rude, and so he concocts an excuse to extricate himself from the Boor's clutches. He claims to be on his way to visit a sick friend a far distance away—to no avail.

Our attention in "Act 2" (lines 23–43) focuses on the incessantly babbling Boor. In an effort to win Horace's esteem, he claims unwittingly to possess precisely those qualities that Horace was known to denounce—singing, dancing, and speedy writing. Horace makes clear to the reader his annoyance and frustration at his own predicament by revealing a prophecy given to him in his youth—that he would meet his end not as a result of sickness or violence, but by exposure to a talker. A glimmer of hope is quickly squelched when the loquacious hanger-on, unexpectedly summoned to make an appearance in court, decides to forego his case in favor of sticking with Horace.

The plot thickens in "Act 3" (lines 43–74). While Horace may have consoled himself with the thought that he himself was the object of this unwanted attention, the real purpose of all the fuss is now apparent. The Boor is patently weaseling his way into an introduction to Horace's patron, Maecenas. Now Horace begins to vent his feelings. He explains indignantly that things are not done that way among his literary friends. At this point, another possible escape route is cut short when Aristius Fuscus, a prankster-friend of Horace, happens upon the scene. He quickly assesses the situation and plays a practical joke. He refuses to acknowledge Horace's thinly-veiled pleas for help and rushes off (surely with a laugh) to perform a pretended obligation.

xvi • Horace Satire 1.9: The Boor

Just as everything looks dim, a solution to Horace's dilemma is brought about swiftly by the resurfacing of the scofflaw's legal troubles in "Act 4" (lines 74–78). The plaintiff and his entourage, with a great deal of noise and confusion, rush up and whisk the Boor off to court. Horace, grateful, relieved and free at last, attributes his salvation to Apollo, the patron of poets.

But if, as has been recently suggested (see Mazurek 1997), Horace must now, because of a legal necessity, accompany the Boor to court as a witness, he is not free yet. In this case, the ending may be taken as ironic—"So *this* is how Apollo saved me!"

Apollo Musagetes (leader of the Muses).
From *Costumes of the Greeks and Romans* by Thomas Hope (New York: Dover, 1962).

Horace Satire 1.9
THE BOOR

1. **Via Sacra:** (ablative of place) "on the Via Sacra." The Via Sacra was the main street of ancient Rome; it ran through the middle of the Forum.

2. **nescio quid ... nugarum:** "I know not what [of] trifles/ ditties; some trifle/ ditty or other." **Nugarum** is a partitive genitive. The word prepares us for the light tone of the satire (cf. Catullus 1.4, *meas esse aliquid putare nugas*).

meditans: used with *nescio quid nugarum*, the sense is "composing light verses," rather than just "thinking about trifles." By informing us that he was composing ditties in his head as he was walking along, Horace plays the part of poet in this satire.

totus in illis: "entirely [absorbed] in them."

3. **quidam:** the "certain person" is never named, although Horace claims here to know his name. Whether the man represents an actual person or is merely a stereotype cannot be determined.

4–5. The quick exchange that takes place in these lines is in the highly colloquial *sermo cotidianus* or everyday speech characteristic of Roman comedy and the neoteric poets. The words of the Boor are, however, slightly more familiar and glib than Horace's somewhat more reserved response. The conversation may be loosely translated:

> "How are things, old pal?"
> "Just fine, at the moment, and I hope all's well with you. If that's all, I'll be on my way?"

accurrit (3) runs up, **arrepta** (4) snatches up, and **adsectaretur** (6) sticks close, form an interesting triad of verbs. The repetition of the prefix *ad-* underscores the idea of aggressive urgency, a sort of encroachment upon personal space on the part of the Boor.

4. **dulcissime rerum:** another partitive genitive.

5. **inquam, 'et cupio omnia ... ':** the double elision alerts us to the rapidity with which Horace hopes to dispatch the fellow.

6. **Cum adsectaretur:** again, the elision, emphatically placed at the beginning of the line, calls attention to Horace's haste to be rid of the Boor.

Num quid vis?: a dismissive sort of question, expecting no response.

Horace uses **occupo** in the sense of "I beat him to it."

At = but, although it is stronger than *sed*, emphasizing the fact that the Boor just doesn't catch on that Horace wants nothing more to do with him.

Satire 1.9

The text for *Satire* 1.9 follows the OCT (Wickham/ Garrod) edition. Changes have been made in capitalization to conform with common English usage. In line 23 the accusative plural *pluris* has been changed to *plures*; likewise in lines 28 and 48 *omnis* to *omnes*, and in line 56 *difficilis* to *difficiles*. Single quotation marks have been changed to double for the sake of legibility.

    Ibam forte Via Sacra, sicut meus est mos,
    nescio quid meditans nugarum, totus in illis.
    Accurrit quidam notus mihi nomine tantum,
    arreptaque manu "Quid agis, dulcissime rerum?"
5   "Suaviter, ut nunc est," inquam, "et cupio omnia quae vis."
    Cum adsectaretur, "Num quid vis?" occupo. At ille
    "Noris nos" inquit; "docti sumus." Hic ego "Pluris
    hoc" inquam "mihi eris." Misere discedere quaerens,
    ire modo ocius, interdum consistere, in aurem
10 dicere nescio quid puero, cum sudor ad imos

7. **Noris** = *noveris* (SYNCOPE). In fact, the fellow has taken Horace's previous question literally. We can supply the words *volo ut* as an ELLIPSIS, "[Yes, I do want something]—I want that you know me."

docti sumus: *doctus* was a term espoused by the neoterics; it implied that a person was generally cultured and literary. The use of the plural here is an affectation.

Pluris: (genitive of value with **eris**) you will be [worth] more.

8. **hoc:** (ablative) because of this, i.e., because you are cultured. A sarcastic remark, apparently lost on the Boor.

9–10. A good example of how meter enhances words. The two opening dactyls, corresponding to the words **ire modo ocius**, hurry the reader along, as Horace hurries. The next two spondees, before the dactyl that is usually found in the fifth foot, force the reader to slow down as the sense of **interdum consistere** demands.

ire, consistere, dicere: (historical infinitives) "I went, I stopped short, I said."

10. **puero:** an attendant, known as a *pedisequus*, who accompanied a distinguished citizen. A slave was commonly referred to as a *puer*, regardless of his age.

10–11. Ad imos manaret talos: the ENJAMBEMENT enhances the visual image of sweat dripping down to Horace's ankles as the words "drip down" into the next line.

11–12. te ... felicem: (accusative of exclamation) "you, fortunate ... !"

Bolane: (vocative) the APOSTROPHE to Bolanus, a man who, we can presume, was known for his hot-headedness, creates the desired mock-dramatic/histrionic effect. Bolanus may have been associated with the town of Bolae in Latium. Livy (4.49–50) tells of events surrounding the Romans' violent occupation of the community of Bolae in the fifth century B.C.E.

cerebri felicem: *cerebrum*, the brain or skull, was also considered the seat of intelligence and the seat of anger. Following Greek usage (cf. Aristophanes, *The Knights*, 186), it can mean "hotheadedness"; *felix* is frequently followed by the genitive, hence "fortunate in (of) your hotheadedness."

12. tacitus: under his breath. Horace's words are clearly not meant for the Boor to hear. The word hints at a dramatic "aside," with which Horace cleverly admits his readers into the theater of his private thoughts.

12–13. cum ille ... vicos, urbem laudaret: The ASYNDETON in **vicos, urbem** emphasizes the ongoing nature of the Boor's verbal ramblings as it simultaneously expresses Horace's desire to cut them short. The imperfect subjunctive of **laudaret** is used here with **cum** to express causality.

Augustus was said to have found a city of bricks and left a city of marble. Presumably the Boor had just cause to praise the city's works-in-progress as he walked downtown and through the Forum. In his *Res Gestae*, Augustus mentions that he completed buildings which had been begun by Julius Caesar, for example, the Curia and the Basilica Julia in the Forum, and the Forum Julium adjacent to it. When this satire was published, between 38 and 35 B.C.E, work on these and other buildings and monuments was underway.

14–16. The Boor speaks in short, clipped sentences. He has discovered Horace's distaste for his company, and tersely states his intention to accompany him.

15. nil agis: "it's no use."

17–18. In an effort to rid himself of the Boor, Horace pretends that he is going to visit a sick friend who lives across the Tiber. (**Trans Tiberim** refers to the area of Rome known today as Trastevere.) What could be less appealing to his unwanted companion, he hopes, than walking a far distance to visit a sick person he doesn't even know? Horace's word order suggests the unfolding of his lie. First he says **trans Tiberim longe**, emphasizing the distance, then **cubat**, the friend is lying in bed (he must be rather sick, maybe even contagious), and finally, almost as an afterthought, the weak pronoun **is**, the person himself, about whom Horace says nothing since he doesn't really exist.

manaret talos. "O te, Bolane, cerebri
felicem!" aiebam tacitus, cum quidlibet ille
garriret, vicos, urbem laudaret. Ut illi
nil respondebam, "Misere cupis" inquit "abire;
15 iamdudum video: sed nil agis; usque tenebo;
persequar hinc quo nunc iter est tibi." "Nil opus est te
circumagi: quendam volo visere non tibi notum:
trans Tiberim longe cubat is, prope Caesaris hortos."
"Nil habeo quod agam et non sum piger: usque sequar te."
20 Demitto auriculas, ut iniquae mentis asellus,
cum gravius dorso subiit onus. Incipit ille:
"Si bene me novi non Viscum pluris amicum,

• •

20. Demitto auriculas: By comparing himself to an unwilling donkey with drooping ears, Horace is punning on his own *cognomen*, Flaccus or "Flap-ear."

21. dorso: ablative with *subiit*.

The image of Horace as a defeated and long-suffering little ass brings "Act 1" of our drama to a close. Appropriately, "Act 2" begins with the word **incipit**.

22. Si bene me novi: Irony abounds in this line. The Boor has appeared to be thick-skinned and unaware of Horace's hints. And yet, when in lines 14–15 he confesses that he has known all along that Horace wants to lose him, we realize that he is more perceptive than he seems. In fact, we now suspect that he has masterminded an elaborate plan and that he knows himself very well indeed. The Boor's remark here is perhaps an allusion to the famous inscription at the Temple of Apollo at Delphi, "Know thyself." If so, the allusion would introduce Apollo, the god of prophecy, patron of poets and a favorite of Horace. We will encounter both prophecy and a further reference to Apollo later in the poem.

22–23. Viscus, Varius, and **Fuscus** (61): three literary friends of Horace. In *Satire* 10.81–3, Horace expresses the hope that he will please them. The suggestion that the Boor will become as good a friend to Horace as are Viscus and Varius is quite outrageous, especially since it was Varius who, along with Vergil, helped secure for Horace an introduction to Maecenas.

22. pluris: genitive of value with **amicum.**

23–25. Ironically, the Boor drives a nail into his own coffin when he suggests that he can write copious verses quickly, an activity that Horace was known to deplore. He also claims to dance gracefully and to sing as well as Hermogenes, perhaps the same person whom Horace criticizes in *Satires* 3 and 10. Note the ALLITERATIVE and self-satisfied *m* sound in **membra movere mollius**.

26. Interpellandi locus hic erat: reminiscent of *occupo* (6) and emphasizing again how much the fellow talks.

26–27. While the apparently abrupt change of subject may remind a modern reader of the cliché, "Don't I hear your mother calling you?" upon closer reading, Horace is probably referring to the Boor's arrogant boasts and suggests that Nemesis may take revenge on him (cf. Catullus 50.20), causing his family to suffer the loss of his support (see Brown 78). It could also be an allusion to the risk of exposing himself to contagion if he accompanies Horace to the home of the sick friend (see Rudd 284, n. 41).

26. tibi: dative of possession.

27. quis = *quibus*, dative of person(s) in need with **est opus.**

te salvo: ablative to agree with **te,** ablative of person needed. **Quis te salvo est opus** can be translated literally "for whom you [being] safe is necessary," or loosely "to whom your safety is important."

28. omnes composui: "I have buried them all [placed their remains]." The mention of placing remains or ashes in a funerary urn brings back Horace's childhood memory of the old woman shaking her lot-filled urn (29–30).

28–34. Horace's second aside begins with the word **felices**, a mock-epic APOSTROPHE. The mock-epic tone continues through the quoting of the prophecy.

29. Sabella: this adjective refers to early Italic tribes who spoke a form of Oscan. Eventually the Samnites emerged as the most powerful of these Oscan-speakers and in Augustan poetic usage the adjective Sabellian is synonymous with Samnite.

30. puero: (ablative absolute) "when I was a boy."

The translation of the words **divina mota anus urna**, sometimes found with the first two words transposed (**mota divina anus urna**), present something of a challenge. There are those who see a three-word ablative absolute in **mota divina urna**, with **divina** interpreted as a TRANSFERRED EPITHET (after the divine urn had been shaken), and those who take **divina** as a nominative agreeing with **anus** (the godlike [Sabellian] old woman [sang] after the urn had been shaken). Because the final *a* of **divina** is elided, we cannot be sure of its quantity.

31–34. The stately language in these lines differs vastly from the *sermo cotidianus* that precedes. Here the hexameters take on a more formal, epic-sounding tone,

non Varium facies: nam quis me scribere plures
aut citius possit versus? Quis membra movere
25 mollius? Invideat quod et Hermogenes ego canto."
Interpellandi locus hic erat: "Est tibi mater,
cognati, quis te salvo est opus?" "Haud mihi quisquam:
omnes composui." "Felices! Nunc ego resto.
Confice; namque instat fatum mihi triste, Sabella
30 quod puero cecinit divina mota anus urna:
Hunc neque dira venena nec hosticus auferet ensis,
nec laterum dolor aut tussis, nec tarda podagra;
garrulus hunc quando consumet cumque: loquaces,
si sapiat, vitet, simul atque adoleverit aetas."
35 Ventum erat ad Vestae, quarta iam parte diei

• •

as befits the mock-heroic seriousness of the prophet's words, and enhance the suggestion of prophecy introduced with "**Si bene me novi**" (line 22). Highly figurative, these four lines contain ANAPHORA (**neque ... nec ... nec**), TRANSFERRED EPITHET, PERSONIFICATION (**tarda podagra**), TMESIS (**quando ... cumque**), and ASSONANCE (**atque adoleverit aetas**).

35. Ventum erat: though the impersonal use of *venio* is common and appropriate in this context, it has been suggested (Rudd 77) that Horace, in opting not to use the first person plural *venimus*, is avoiding even a grammatical association between himself and the Boor. Furthermore, Rudd notes that in the entire satire Horace uses the first person plural only twice, in *vivimus* (48), with Maecenas and his friends as the subject, and in *consistimus* (62), with Horace and Fuscus as the subject.

ad Vestae = **ad** [*aedem* (shrine)] **Vestae.** Since Horace and his companion are walking along the Via Sacra, and are now at the shrine of Vesta in the Forum, they are also near the Basilica Julia, where legal matters were treated.

quarta ... parte diei: the Roman day was divided into twelve "hours," consisting not of sixty minutes each, but of one-twelfth of the available daylight. Thus, during the winter months an "hour" comprised fewer than sixty minutes and in summer, more. The first hour of the day for a Roman was roughly comparable to our 6:00 to 7:00 A.M. When Horace says that one quarter of the day was gone, we can therefore surmise that it was now sometime after 9:00 A.M., the time when the business day began and the courts were in session.

36–37. As will be made clear in lines 74–78, the Boor is a debtor who has been taken to court by a creditor. Apparently the court proceedings have not been concluded. According to Roman legal practice, at the time of adjournment, the debtor (defendant) had to promise to reappear to complete the proceedings when summoned. To guarantee his reappearance, he was required to post a bond. Now it is after 9:00 A.M. on the day the Boor has agreed to present himself in court. He has three choices: he can abandon Horace in order to meet his legal obligation; he can ask Horace to go to court on his behalf as a *vindex*, or guarantor, to bring about a further postponement of the proceedings (this would place Horace under financial obligations should the fellow fail to show up again); or he can risk losing his bond and worry about the whole thing at a later time. Civil duty becomes a metaphor for proper social behavior, the tenets of which the Boor clearly chooses to ignore.

36. casu: "by chance," as luck would have it.

vadato: (ablative absolute) "having posted a bond."

37. quod ni fecisset, perdere litem: it should be noted that Horace is in error when he says that if the Boor didn't show up, he would lose his suit. This may be cleverly intentional on Horace's part since he claims only two lines later that he doesn't know civil law. The antecedent of **quod** is the clause **casu tum respondere vadato debebat. Debebat** is to be understood as the main verb that governs the complementary infinitive **perdere**, "if he didn't do this, he must forfeit his case."

38. Si me amas: Literally, "if you love me," a formulaic expression that may be translated as "please."

38–40. Horace gives three reasons for refusing to serve as *vindex*: that he does not have the financial wherewithal (**interea m si aut valeo**); that he is not well versed in civil law (**aut novi civilia iura**); and, almost as an afterthought, that he is in a hurry, leaving "to visit his sick friend" implied but not said (**et propero quo scis**).

41. sodes = *si audes,* "if you dare." Colloquial for "please" (cf Catullus 103.1).

42–43. Just as "Act 1" ended with the representation of Horace as an unwilling donkey, so "Act 2" concludes with a metaphor of Horace as a foe acknowledging defeat and acquiescing to march behind a triumphant general. The comparison is all the more fitting since Horace and the Boor are walking through the Forum on the Via Sacra, a portion of the triumphal route that culminated at the Temple of Jupiter Optimus Maximus on the Capitoline Hill.

43. "Act 3" begins with a zinger when the Boor bluntly asks, **"Maecenas quomodo tecum?"** ("How do you and Maecenas get on?") Now the truth is out. Hitherto Horace could have flattered himself that, unappreciated as the Boor's advances

praeterita, et casu tunc respondere vadato
debebat; quod ni fecisset, perdere litem.
"Si me amas" inquit "paulum hic ades." "Interream si
aut valeo stare aut novi civilia iura;
40 et propero quo scis." "Dubius sum quid faciam" inquit,
"tene relinquam an rem." "Me, sodes." "Non faciam" ille,
et praecedere coepit. Ego, ut contendere durum est
cum victore, sequor. "Maecenas quomodo tecum?"

• •

may have been, they at least indicated sincere admiration for Horace's own abilities as a poet. Now Horace realizes that he is just a steppingstone to the real prize, his patron Maecenas.

Maecenas: Gaius Maecenas was one of Augustus' oldest and most trusted friends and advisors. Of Etruscan ancestry, he was a member of the equestrian rank. His wealth, extravagant taste, and sumptuous lifestyle were legendary. Maecenas became the literary patron of some of the greatest writers of Latin literature, including Propertius and Vergil, who introduced Horace to him. Horace dedicated his first book of satires, his epodes, his first three books of odes, and his first book of epistles to Maecenas. Maecenas gave Horace the Sabine Farm, his beloved refuge and retreat from the complications of life in the city of Rome. Both men died in the same year—8 B.C.E.

Discussion about the role of the literary patron in ancient Rome, especially regarding the amount of influence he exerted over those he supported, continues to spark debate. Peter White, who prefers to refer to Maecenas and his group as a "network of friends" (41) is cautious about the use of the more common phrase "the circle of Maecenas." He says:

> Important persons in Roman society certainly attracted other men whose movements came to revolve around their own. If that is all it means to talk about the "circle of Maecenas," the figure does no harm. But if it has an ideological overtone, implying that Maecenas was the source of the projects, causes, and directions pursued by his writer friends, that proposition calls for challenge and ultimately rejection (White 38).

44. repetit: apparently Horace is so taken off guard that he is speechless, for the Boor, apparently receiving no answer to his question, repeats or resumes discussion of Maecenas.

44–45. It is not clear whether Horace or his companion speaks the next two sentences, or whether they are spoken by each alternately. By altering the punctuation, the words are appropriate to any combination of speakers. If it is the Boor who speaks both sentences, they can be taken to mean "[I hear that he is a man] of few friends and of sharp mind [and that] no one has used good fortune more handily." Remove the elliptical "I hear that" and the statement could equally convincingly be spoken by Horace.

46. adiutorem: a helper, but also used as a technical term for an assistant in the imperial household. The Boor suggests that he would help Horace gain favors if he were part of the group.

46. secundas: "second," and by extension, "favorable" (as a "second" wind).

47. tradere: in a metaphorical sense, it can mean "to teach." The double meaning is appropriate: "I'll be a help to you if you teach me [how to be a good poet/ how to act with Maecenas]," or "if you hand me over (i.e., just let me in)."

48. summosses = *summovisses,* [SYNCOPE] used to describe the motion of a lictor who "sweeps away" any obstacles from the path of the magistrate he precedes and protects. The pluperfect subjunctive here gives the sense "may I perish (I'll be damned) if you would not have (already) cleared the path of all (competitors in Maecenas' group on your behalf)."

isto: this word has a harsher (hissing) sound and a more pejorative meaning than *illo*.

49. rere = *reris*.

hac: ablative of comparison, "no house [i.e., that of Maecenas] is more faultless than this one."

50. magis his aliena malis: "[no house] is more foreign to these intrigues."

his. . . malis (dative with **aliena**) refers to the bad behavior and intrigues that the Boor has suggested abound among Maecenas' friends.

nil mi[hi] officit: "it makes no difference to me."

52. Magnum narras: "your story is hard to believe; you tell a tall tale."

53–54. Horace had hoped that by setting the Boor straight about the way things were with Maecenas and his friends, he would dash his hopes of entry into the group. The truth, however, has had the opposite effect.

hinc repetit: "Paucorum hominum et mentis bene sanae;
45   nemo dexterius fortuna est usus. Haberes
magnum adiutorem, posset qui ferre secundas,
hunc hominem velles si tradere: dispeream ni
summosses omnes." "Non isto vivimus illic
quo tu rere modo; domus hac nec purior ulla est
50   nec magis his aliena malis; nil mi officit" inquam
"ditior hic aut est quia doctior; est locus uni
cuique suus." "Magnum narras, vix credibile." "Atqui
sic habet." "Accendis, quare cupiam magis illi
proximus esse." "Velis tantummodo, quae tua virtus,
55   expugnabis; et est qui vinci possit, eoque
difficiles aditus primos habet." "Haud mihi dero:
muneribus servos corrumpam; non, hodie si
exclusus fuero, desistam; tempora quaeram;
occurram in triviis; deducam. Nil sine magno
60   vita labore dedit mortalibus." Haec dum agit, ecce

• •

54. Velis tantummodo: a blatantly sarcastic remark on Horace's part, "You have only to wish it" [you are pushy enough to get want you want]. Horace expects the Boor to take this as a compliment—i.e., "You are so talented, I am sure you will succeed."

quae tua virtus: "such is your strength," i.e., you will stop at nothing, or, more sarcastically, "such is your moral perfection."

56. aditus primos: Horace means this in a figurative sense, i.e., first contact with Maecenas. His companion takes it more literally as the first entryway into his house.

56–59. The fellow reveals his plan of attack, which includes bribing Maecenas' slaves, frequent attempts to gain access to the house, and if that fails, waylaying the great man at the crossroads. The Boor characterizes his own efforts as **labor** (59–60). But they are marked instead by offensive and obvious subterfuge, a quality which was actually quite opposed to the Roman virtue of *labor*.

56. dero = *deero*.

59. triviis: "at the crossroads," or the place where three roads converge.

61. **Fuscus Aristius:** a friend of Horace (see n. 22–23 on Viscus) and the addressee of *Odes* 1.22. Horace has reversed the normal order of his names, much as Catullus did in 10.30 (*Cinna est Gaius*). As in Catullus' poem, the narrator's friend fails to stave off an embarrassing and uncomfortable predicament for him.

62. **nosset** = *novisset* [SYNCOPE].

63. **rogat et respondet:** an economical way of explaining that each asks the other the same questions and reponds to them.

64. **lentissima:** "very irresponsive," i.e., although Horace squeezes Aristius' arms, he does not respond.

64–65. **nutans, distorquens oculos:** this reaction is so common that we have little difficulty visualizing Horace's attempt to communicate his predicament to Fuscus. It serves as an effective and humorous sight gag.

65. **Male salsus:** the sense of this phrase is "inappropriately witty" (cf. Catullus 10.33, *insulsa male*).

66. **dissimulare ... urere:** historical infinitives.

meum iecur urere bilis: "bile burns my liver."

69. **tricesima sabbata:** there is no known Jewish holiday of this name, a silly excuse on the part of Fuscus.

vin: Although **vin** is a contraction for *visne*, Bennett suggests that here it expects a negative answer, more like *num vis*.

70. **curtis Iudaeis:** (dative after *oppedere*) "circumcised Jews."

71: **At mihi: mi** = *mihi* (dative of possession). "[You may not have religious scruples,] but I do."

paulo infirmior: "a little weaker," i.e., less able to resist the demands of religion.

72. **alias:** (adverb) "at another time."

72–73. **solem tam nigrum surrexe mihi:** cf. Catullus 8.3 and 8.8, *fulsere quondam candidi tibi soles*.

73. **surrexe** = *surrexisse* [SYNCOPE]. Using an infinitive in an exclamation is common in comedy.

74. **sub cultro:** "under the knife," i.e., as a sacrificial victim or, perhaps, a play on *curtis* (70). Thus, "Act 3" ends with a third image of Horace as victim. Each image has become successively more desperate: the donkey was merely refusing an unpleasant task; the defeated soldier was humiliated; now, as a sacrificial victim, death is imminent for Horace. The first half of the line is spondaic.

Fuscus Aristius occurri, mihi carus et illum
qui pulchre nosset. Consistimus. "Unde venis?" et
"Quo tendis?" rogat et respondet. Vellere coepi,
et prensare manu lentissima bracchia, nutans,
65   distorquens oculos, ut me eriperet. Male salsus
ridens dissimulare: meum iecur urere bilis.
"Certe nescio quid secreto velle loqui te
aiebas mecum." "Memini bene, sed meliore
tempore dicam: hodie tricesima sabbata: vin tu
70   curtis Iudaeis oppedere?" "Nulla mihi" inquam
"religio est." "At mi: sum paulo infirmior, unus
multorum: ignosces: alias loquar." Huncine solem
tam nigrum surrexe mihi! Fugit improbus ac me
sub cultro linquit. Casu venit obvius illi
75   adversarius et "Quo tu turpissime?" magna
inclamat voce, et "Licet antestari?" Ego vero

Casu: as in line 36, the Boor's brush with the law this second time was unexpected.

75. adversarius: the creditor (plaintiff) in the lawsuit referred to in lines 36–7. Apparently he was not satisfied to win his case by default and now demands the presence of the Boor in court.

76. Licet antestari: "May I ask you to stand as witness?" According to the laws of the Twelve Tables, if a defendant refused to go when summoned, he could be

Temple of Vesta in the Roman Forum (see line 35). Photo by M. A. Brucia.

oppono auriculam. Rapit in ius: clamor utrimque:
undique concursus. Sic me servavit Apollo.

••

77. oppono auriculam: "I put out my ear [to be touched]." According to Pliny the Elder (*Natural History* 11.251) the earlobe was a *locus memoriae*, a place on the body where memory was stored. Horace offers his ear to be touched by the plaintiff, signifying that he will not forget that he agreed to serve as a witness to the seizure of the Boor.

77–78. clamor utrimque: undique concursus: ELLIPSIS, CHIASMUS, and ENJAMBEMENT. Note the difference in meaning between **utrimque** and **undique**. "[There is] shouting on both sides (they shout at each other) and there is a running together of people from all directions."

The Romans had a custom called *flagitatio*, a verbal pelting, whereby a person who had not received his due, a creditor, for instance, would embarrass his debtor by assembling a crowd of people to hunt him down and abuse him verbally in a public place such as the Forum. It was hoped that fear of further defamation and humiliation would encourage the debtor to fulfill his obligation (see Fraenkel 1958).

It is, of course, ironic that the Boor, Horace's relentless besieger, in the end becomes the besieged.

78. Sic me servavit Apollo: Horace's *deus ex machina* is Apollo, who has come to his rescue after all. The Boor did not know himself well enough to worm his way into the charmed circle!

If, as has been argued (see Mazurek 1997), Horace must accompany the Boor to court as a witness immediately, the ending is doubly ironic. Instead of a statement of fact, "Thus Apollo saved me," the final sentence may be interpreted sarcastically by placing more emphasis on **Sic**—"*Thus* Apollo saved me!" Horace's dealings with the Boor would continue in the courtroom.

Statue of Horace in main square, Venosa. Photo by M. A. Brucia.

Glossary of Terms

These terms are used in the Notes on the Text; this list is not exhaustive.

ALLITERATION: the repetition of a sound or a letter, often an initial consonant (lines 23–25).

ANAPHORA: the repetition of a word or similar words at the start of a sentence or clause (**neque ... nec ... Nec,** lines 31–34).

APOSTROPHE: an address to an absent person or personification, suddenly and in the middle of some other discourse (**O ... Bolane,** lines 11–12).

ASSONANCE: the repetition of vowel sounds (**atque adoleverit aetas,** line 34).

ASYNDETON: the lack of or omission of connective words where they would otherwise be expected (**vicos, urbem,** line 13).

CHIASMUS: a word order whereby similar words or structures are positioned in the pattern of ABBA (lines 77–78, **clamor utrimque:undique concursus**).

ELLIPSIS: words, usually verbs, omitted but implied (line 7).

ENJAMBEMENT: the spilling over of a thought to the next line (lines 10–11).

PERSONIFICATION: treatment of an inanimate object or a concept as a person (**tarda podagra,** line 32).

SYNCOPE: the omission of a syllable in the middle of a word, common in past tense forms (**noris** for **noveris,** line 7).

TMESIS: the separation of a compound word into two distinct parts by an intervening word or words (**quando ... cumque,** line 33).

TRANSFERRED EPITHET: a word which agrees grammatically with one word but better describes another (**divina ... urna,** line 30, describes not the urn but the old woman).

Inscription identifying Horace as the composer of the Carmen Saeculare. Courtesy Fototeca Unione, American Academy in Rome.

Bibliography

Text
Wickham, E. C. *Q. Horati Flacci Opera.* Second edition. Edited by H. W. Garrod. Oxford: Clarendon Press, 1963.

Commentaries
Bennett, Charles E. and John Carew Rolfe. *Horace: The Complete Works.* Boston, New York, and Chicago: Allyn and Bacon, 1901.

Brown, Michael P. *Horace: Satires I.* Warminster, England: Aris and Phillips, 1993.

Lejay, P. *Oeuvres d'Horace: Satires.* Paris: Libraire Hachette, 1911.

Morris, Edward P. *Horace: Satires and Epistles.* Norman, OK: University of Oklahoma Press, 1967 [1969].

Palmer, Arthur. *The Satires of Horace.* Fourth edition. New York: Macmillan and Co., 1891.

Paoli, Ugo Enrico. *Satire, Epistole.* Firenze: Felice LeMonnier, 1967.

Translations of Horace
Bovie, Smith Palmer. *Satires and Epistles. A Modern Verse Translation.* Chicago: University of Chicago Press, 1959.

Fairclough, H. Rushton. *Horace: Satires, Epistles and Ars Poetica.* The Loeb Classical Library. Cambridge, MA: Harvard University Press, 1970.

Passage, Charles E. *The Complete Works of Horace.* New York: Frederick Ungar Publishing Co., 1983.

Rudd, Niall. *The Satires of Horace and Persius.* New York: Penguin Classics, 1974.

Other
Anderson, William S. *Essays on Roman Satire.* Princeton: Princeton University Press, 1982.

Armstrong, David. *Horace*. New Haven and London: Yale University Press, 1989.

Berger, Adolf. *Encyclopedic Dictionary of Roman Law*. Philadelphia: The American Philosophical Society, 1953.

Braund, S. H. *Roman Verse Satire*. Greece and Rome New Surveys in the Classics, No. 23. Oxford: Oxford University Press, 1992.

Braund, Susanna Morton. *The Roman Satirists and their Masks*. London: Bristol Classical Press, 1996.

Coffey, Michael. *Roman Satire*. London: Methuen and Co. New York: Barnes and Noble, 1976.

Conte, Gian Biagio. *Latin Literature: A History*. Trans. by Joseph B. Solodow. Revised by Don Fowler and Glenn W. Most. Baltimore: The Johns Hopkins University Press, 1994. (Originally published as *Letteratura latina: Manuale storico dalle origini alla fine dell'impero romano*, Florence: Le Monnier, 1987).

Courtney, E. W., ed. *The Fragmentary Latin Poets*. With Commentary. Oxford: Clarendon Press, 1993.

———. "Horace and the Pest," *Classical Journal* 90 (1994) 1–8.

Crook, J. A. *Law and Life of Rome*. London and Southampton: The Camelot Press, 1967.

Duff, J. Wight. *Roman Satire: Its Outlook on Social Life*. Berkeley: University of California Press, 1936.

Ferry, David, trans. *The Odes of Horace*. New York: Farrar, Strauss and Giroux, 1998.

Fraenkel, Eduard. "Two Poems of Catullus." *Journal of Roman Studies* 48 (1958) 46–53.

———. *Horace*. Oxford: Clarendon Press, 1957.

Freudenburg, Kirk. *The Walking Muse: Horace on the Theory of Satire*. Princeton: Princeton University Press, 1993.

Galinsky, Karl. *Augustan Culture*. Princeton: Princeton University Press, 1996.

Gold, Barbara K., ed. *Literary and Artistic Patronage in Greece and Rome*. Austin: University of Texas Press, 1982.

———. *Literary Patronage in Greece and Rome*. Chapel Hill: University of North Carolina Press, 1987.

Griffin, Jasper. *Latin Poets and Roman Life*. Chapel Hill: University of North Carolina Press, 1986.

Haynes, Kenneth, and D. S. Carne-Ross, eds. *Horace in English*. Reprint edition. New York: Penquin USA, 1996.

Henderson, John. "Be Alert (Your Country Needs Lerts): Horace, *Satires* 1.9," *Proceedings of the Cambridge Philological Society* 39 (1993) 67–93.

Highet, Gilbert. *Anatomy of Satire*. Princeton: Princeton University Press, 1962.

Homage to Horace: A Bimillenary Celebration. Ed. by S. J. Harrison. Oxford: Clarendon Press, 1995. Especially recommended: Harrison, "Some Twentieth-century Views of Horace," 1–16, and Gordon Williams, "*Libertino patre natus*: True or False," 296–313.

Knoche, Ulrich. *Roman Satire*. Translated by Edwin S. Ramage. Bloomington and London: Indiana University Press, 1975.

Levi, Peter. *Horace: A Life*. London: Duckworth, 1997.

Lyne, R. O. A. M. *Horace: Behind the Public Poetry*. New Haven: Yale University Press, 1995.

Martindale, Charles, and David Hopkins, eds. *Horace Made New: Horatian Influences on British Writing from the Renaissance to the Twentieth Century*. Cambridge, MA: Cambridge University Press, 1993.

Mazurek, Tadeusz. "Self-parody and the Law in Horace's *Satires* 1.9." *Classical Journal* 93 (1997) 1–17.

Mendell, Clarence W. *Latin Poetry: The New Poets and the Augustans*. New Haven and London: Yale University Press, 1965.

Oberhelman, Steven, and David Armstrong. "Satire as Poetry and the Impossibility of Metathesis in Horace's *Satires*." In *Philodemus and Poetry*. Edited by Dirk Obbink. New York and Oxford: Oxford University Press, 1995.

Quintilian. *Institutio Oratoria*, 4 vols. Trans. by H. E. Butler. The Loeb Classical Library. Cambridge, MA: Harvard University Press, 1959–1963.

Ramage, Edwin S., David L. Sigsbee, and Sigmund C. Fredericks. *Roman Satirists and their Satire: The Fine Art of Criticism in Ancient Rome*. Park Ridge, NJ: Noyes Press, 1974.

Reckford, Kenneth J. *Horace*. New York: Twayne Publishers, 1969.

Remains of Old Latin, 4 vols. Ed. and trans. by E. H. Warmington. The Loeb Classical Library. Cambridge, MA: Harvard University Press, 1961–1967.

Rudd, Niall, ed. *Horace 2000: A Celebration*. Ann Arbor: University of Michigan Press, 1993.

Rudd, Niall. *The Satires of Horace*. Cambridge: The University Press, 1966.

———. *Themes in Roman Satire*. London: Duckworth, 1986.

Santirocco, Matthew, ed. "Recovering Horace." *Classical World* 87.5 (1994).

Shackleton Bailey, D. R. *Profile of Horace*. Cambridge, MA: Harvard University Press, 1982.

Suetonius. *De Viris Illustribus* and *De Vita Caesarum,* 2 vols. Trans. by J. C. Rolfe. The Loeb Classical Library. Cambridge, MA: Harvard University Press, 1913–1914.

White, Peter. *Promised Verse: Poets in the Society of Augustan Rome*. Cambridge, MA and London: Harvard University Press, 1993.

Williams, Gordon. *Horace*. Oxford: Clarendon Press, 1972. (*Greece and Rome New Surveys in the Classics* no. 6).

———. *The Nature of Roman Poetry*. Oxford: Clarendon Press, 1983.

———. *Tradition and Originality in Roman Poetry*. Oxford: Clarendon Press, 1968.

Vocabulary

A
abeō, abīre, abīvī, abitum: *to depart, to vanish*
ac: conj., *and*
accendō, accendere, accendī, accēnsum: *to set on fire, to stir up*
accurrō, accurrere, accurrī, accursum: *to run up (to)*
ad: prep. w. acc., *to, towards*
aditus, -ūs, m.: *entrance, entry*
adiūtor, adiūtōris, m.: *helper, assistant*
adolescō, adolescere, adolēvī, adultum: *to mature, to become adult, to grow up*
adsector, -ārī, adsectātus sum: *to follow, to tail after*
adsum, adesse, adfuī: *to be present*
adversārius, -ī, m.: *opponent, adversary*
aetās, aetātis, f.: *age, time of life, generation*
agō, agere, ēgī, actum: *to act, to do*
āiō: *to say, to affirm, to assert*
aliās: adv., *at another time*
aliēnus, -a, -um: *another's, foreign, unsuitable*
amīcus, -ī, m.: *friend*
amō, -āre, -āvī, amātum: *to love, to like greatly*
an: conj., *or*
antestor, -ārī, antestātus sum: *to call as witness*
anus, -ūs, f.: *old woman, crone*
Apollō, Apollinis, m.: *Apollo*
arripiō, arripere, arripuī, arreptum: *to snatch, to seize, to arrest*
asellus, -ī, m.: *little ass*
at: conj., *but, on the other hand*
atque: conj., *also, and, as well as*
atquī: conj., *but, anyhow*
auferō, auferre, abstulī, ablātum: *to remove, to withdraw, to snatch, to steal*
auricula, -ae, f.: *external surface of ear*
auris, -is, f.: *ear*
aut: conj., *or, or rather*

B
bene: adv., *well, quite, thoroughly*
bīlis, bīlis, f.: *gall, bile, wrath, anger*
Bōlānus, -ī, m.: *Bolanus, a man*
brācchium, -ī, n.: *arm, lower arm*

C
Caesar, Caesaris: *Caesar* (here, Augustus)
canō, canere, cecinī, cantum: *to sing, to recite, to perform*
cantō, -āre, -āvī, -ātum: *to sing, to recite, to perform*
cārus, -a, -um: *dear, beloved, expensive*
cāsus, -ūs, m.: *case, event, mishap,* (abl.) *by chance*
cerebrum, -ī, n.: *brain, the seat of intelligence or the senses, the seat of anger, anger, hotheadedness*
certē: adv., *certainly, surely*
circumagō, circumagere, circumēgī, circumactum: *to turn around, to sway*
citius: compar. adv., *more quickly*
cīvīlis, -e: adj., *civil, polite*
clāmor, clāmōris, m.: *outcry, outburst*
coepī, coepisse: defective vb., *I begin, I have begun*
cognātus, -a, -um: *related, similar*
compōnō, compōnere, composuī,

compositum: *to put away, to lay aside, to bury, to appease*
concursus, -ūs, m.: *collision, running together*
conficiō, conficere, confēcī, confectum: *to construct, to prepare, to cause, to fulfil, to finish*
consistō, consistere, constitī, constitum: *to stop, to pause, to halt,* (mil.) *to take up a position*
consūmō, consūmere, consūmpsī, consūmptum: *to consume, to use up*
contendō, contendere, contendī, contentum: *to assert, to compete, to stretch*
corrumpō, corrumpere, corrūpī, corruptum: *to bribe, to corrupt*
crēdibilis, -e: *believable, credible*
cubō, -āre, cubuī, cubitum: *to lie sick*
cuique: with **ūni-** see **ūnusquisque**
culter, cultrī, m.: *knife; razor*
cum: conj. (w. indic. or subj.), *when, whenever, since, because, although*
cum: prep. w. abl., *with, among, amidst*
-cumque: see **quandōcumque**
cupiō, cupere, cupīvī, cupītum: *to desire, to wish for*
curtus, -a, -um: (w. **Iudaeus**) *shortened, circumcised*

dīco, dīcere, dixī, dictum: *to say, to tell, to talk*
diēs, -ēī, m.: *day*
difficilis, -e: *difficult*
dīrus, -a, -um: *dreadful, fearsome, dire*
dīs, dītis: *wealthy, rich; profitable*
discēdō, -ere, discessī, discessum: *to depart, to dispense, to scatter, to break off*
dispereō, disperīre, disperiī: *to go to ruin, to perish*
dissimulō, -āre, āvī, ātum: *to feign*
distorqueō, distorquēre, distorsī, distortum: *to twist, to curl, to roll, to deform*
dīvīnus, -a, -um: *divine, godlike; heaven-sent*
dō, dare, dedī, datum: *to give, to offer, to pay*
doctus, -a, -um: *experienced, learned, clever*
dolor, dolōris, m : *pain, grief, sorrow*
domus, -ūs, f.: *house, home, household*
dorsum, -ī, n.: *ridge; back*
dubius, -a, -um: *doubtful, dubious, chancy*
dulcis, -e: *sweet, kind, pleasant*
dum: conj., *while, as long as*
dūrus, -a, -um: *harsh, severe*

D

dēbeō, dēbēre, dēbuī, dēbitum: *to owe,* (w. inf.) *to be obliged*
dēdūcō, dēdūcere, dēdūxī, dēductum: *to escort, to lead down, to summon*
dēmittō, -ere, dēmīsī, dēmissus: *to drop, to let drop*
dēerō: see **desum**
dēsistō, dēsistere, dēstitī, dēstitum: *to stop, to cease*
dēsum, dēesse, dēfuī: *to be lacking*
dexter, dextera, dexterum: *on the right side, lucky*

E

ecce: interj., *look!, see!*
ego: pers. pron., *I*
ensis, -is, m.: *sword*
eō: adv., *on that account*
eō, īre, īvī, itum: *to go, to depart*
ēripiō, ēripere, ēripuī, ēreptum: *to snatch away*
et: conj. & adv., *even; and*
exclūdō, exclūdere, exclūsī, exclūsum: *to shut out, to remove*
expugnō, -āre, -āvī, -ātum: *to achieve, to conquer*

F

faciō, facere, fēcī, factum: *to make, to do, to perform, to create*
fātum, -ī, n.: *divine oracle, fate, destiny*
fēlix, fēlīcis: *happy, fruitful, lucky*
ferō, ferre, tulī, lātum: *to carry, to bear, to endure, to report*
forte: adv., *by chance*
fortūna, -ae, f.: *chance, fortune, good luck*
fugiō, fugere, fūgī, fugitum: *to flee, to escape*
Fuscus Aristius: *an acquaintance of Horace*

G

garriō, -īre, -īvī: *to chatter, to prattle*
garrulus, -a, -um: *talkative, babbling*
gravis -e: *heavy*

H

habeō, habēre, habuī, habitum: *to have,* (impersonally w. adv.) *to be a certain way*
haud: adv., *not, hardly, not at all, by no means*
Hermogenēs, Hermogenis, m.: *Hermogenes (a writer)*
hīc: adv., *here, in this place, at this point*
hic, haec, hoc: dem. pron. & adj., *this, the actual, the former*
hinc: adv., *from here, on this side*
hodiē: adv., *today, nowadays*
homō, hominis, m./f.: *human being, person, individual*
hortus, -ī, m.: *garden*
hosticus, -a, -um: *hostile, foreign, strange*
huncine: see **hic, haec, hoc** (emphatic form)

I/J

iam: adv., *now, present, already*
iamdūdum: adv., *long ago, long since* (often written as two words)
iecur, iecoris, n.: *liver*
ignoscō, ignoscere, ignōvī, ignōtum: *to pardon, to forgive, to excuse*
ille, illa, illud: dem. pron. & adj., *that, the former, the latter*
illīc: adv., *in that place, over there*
īmus, -a, -um: *bottom of*
improbus, -a, -um: *wicked, inferior, merciless, persistent*
in: prep., (w. abl.) *in, on;* (w. acc.) *into, onto*
incipiō, incipere, incēpī, inceptum: *to begin, to start*
inclāmō, -āre, -āvī, -ātum: *to shout at, to scold*
infirmus, -a, -um: *unwell, faint, weak*
iniquus, -a, -um: *discontented*
inquam: postpositive defective vb. used in direct speech, *I say;* **inquit:** *it is said, one says*
instō, instāre, institī: (w. dat.) *to be close to, to pursue closely, to harass*
interdum: adv., *sometimes, meanwhile*
intereō, interīre, interiī, interitum: *to be done for, to perish*
interpellō, -āre, -āvī, -ātum: *to interrupt, to break in on*
invideō, -ēre, invīdī, invīsum: *to hate, to envy, to cast an evil eye on*
is, ea, id: pers. pron. & dem. adj., *he, she, it, this, that,*
iste, ista, istud: adj., *that of yours; that particular*
iter, itineris, n.: *journey, day's march, walk*
Iūdaeus, -ī, m.: *Jew*
iūs, iūris, n.: *law, case, courtroom*

L

labor, labōris, m.: *toil, work, labor*
latus, lateris, n.: *side, flank, body*
laudō, -āre, -āvī, -ātum: *to praise*

lentus, -a, -um: *sticky, limber, slow, irresponsive*
licet, licēre, licuit or **licitum est:** impers. vb., *it is permitted, it is lawful*
linquō, linquere, līquī: *to leave, to abandon, to forsake*
līs, lītis, f.: *lawsuit, litigation, wrangle*
locus, -ī, m.: *place, site, spot*
longē: adv., *far, far away, greatly, distant*
loquax, loquācis: *talkative, garrulous*
loquor, loquī, locūtus sum: *to speak, to talk*

M

Maecēnās, Maecēnātis, m.: *Maecenas, Horace's patron*
magis: compar. adv., *greater, more*
magnus, -a, -um: *large, great, loud, long (time)*
male: adv., *imperfectly; not; badly; wrongfully*
malus, -a, -um: *bad; evil; unlucky*
manō, -āre, -āvī: *to drip*
manus, -ūs, f.: *hand*
māter, mātris, f.: *mother*
mēcum: mē + cum, see **ego**
meditor, -ārī, -ātus sum: *to think over, reflect on*
melior, melius: (compar. of **bonus**) *better*
membrum, -ī, n.: *limb, member, part*
meminī, meminisse: defective vb., *I remember*
mens, mentis, f.: *mind, wit, opinion, courage*
meus, -a, -um: *my*
mī: contracted form of **mihi,** see **ego**
miserē: adv., *wretchedly, unhappily*
modo: adv. *now and again*
modus, -ī, m.: *way, habit, measure, manner, standard*
mollius: compar. adv., *more smoothly*
mortālis, -is, m.: *mortal, human being*
mōs, mōris, m.: *custom, habit, rule*
moveō, -ēre, mōvī, mōtum: *to move, to undertake*
multus, -a, -um: *much, many*
mūnus, mūneris, n.: *service, gift, favor, kindness, duty*

N

nam: conj., *for, for instance, now, on the other hand*
namque: conj., *for surely*
narrō, -āre, -āvī, -ātum: *to tell*
-ne: enclitic, introduces a question expecting a yes or no answer, (w. **an**) *whether*
nec . . . nec: correlative conj., *neither . . . nor*
nēmō, nēminis, m./f.: *nobody*
neque: conj., *and not*
nesciō, -īre, -īvī, -ītum: *to not know, be ignorant,* (w. **quid**) *some . . . or other*
nī: conj., contracted form of **nisi,** *unless, if not*
niger, nigra, nigrum: *black*
nīl: contracted form of **nihil,** *nothing*
nōmen, nōminis, n.: *name*
nōn: adv., *no, not, not by any means*
nōris: see **noscō**
nōs: pers. pron., *we*
noscō, -ere, nōvī: *to become acquainted with, to recognize, to learn*
nōtus, -a, -um: *known*
nūgae, -ārum, f.: *trifles, nonsense, ditties, light verses*
nullus, -a, -um: *no one, none*
num: introduces a question expecting a no answer, *surely . . . not*
numquid: introduces a direct question expecting a no answer, *surely . . . not*
nunc: adv., *now, nowadays, today*
nūtō, -āre, -āvī, -ātum: *to nod, to hesitate*

O

Ō: interj., *oh!*
obvius, -a, -um: *in the way, exposed, accessible*
occupō, -āre, -āvī, -ātum: *occupy, seize, attack*
occurrō, occurrere, occurrī, occursum: *to run up to, to run to meet, to attack*
ōcius: compar. adv., *more swiftly, sooner, more easily, immediately*
oculus, -ī, m.: *eye*
officiō, officere, offēcī, offectum: *to get in the way, to bother*
omnis, -e: *all, every, the whole*
onus, oneris, n.: *burden*
oppēdō, -ere: (w. dat.) *to deride, to mock; to break wind at, to fart in the face of*
oppōnō, opponere, opposuī, oppositum: *to place, to station, to oppose*
opus, operis, n.: (w. **est** + inf.) *it is useful, beneficial* (w. **est** + dat. of person in need and abl. of person or thing needed) *for whom someone or something is necessary*

P

pars, partis, f.: *part*
paucī, -ae, -a: *few*
paulō: *by a little; rather*
paulum: adv., *awhile*
perdō, perdere, perdidī, perditum: *to perish, to be lost*
persequor, persequī, persecūtus sum: *to follow after eagerly*
piger, pigra, pigrum: *lazy*
plūs, plūris: (compar. of **multus**) *more, too much*
podagra, -ae, f.: *arthritis, gout*
possum, posse, potuī: *to be able*
praecēdō, -ere, praecessī, praecessum: *to precede, to lead, to surpass*
praetereō, praeterīre, praeterīvī or **-iī, praeteritum:** *to pass by, to skip, to go beyond*
prensō, -āre, -āvī, -ātum: *to clutch at, to grab*
prīmus, -a, -um: *first*
prope: adv., *nearby, near*
properō, -āre, -āvī: *to hurry*
proximus, -a, -um: *closest, nearest, very near*
puer, -ī, m.: *boy*
pulcher, pulchra, pulchrum: *lovely, pretty*
pūrus, -a, -um: *simple, unadorned, natural, faultless*

Q

quaerō, quaerere, quaesīvī, quaesītum: *to plan, to seek, to require*
quandō: (w. **cumque**) *whenever*
quārē: *why*
quartus, -a -um: *fourth*
-que: enclitic, *and, also*
quī, quae, quod: rel. pron., *who, which*
quia: conj., *because*
quīdam, quaedam, quoddam: *a certain*
quīlibet, quaelibet, quodlibet: *any at all*
quis, quis, quid: interrog. pron., *who? what?*
quisquam, quicquam or **quidquam:** pron., *anyone, anything*
quō: adv., *to where, whither*
quōmodo: interrog. adv., *in what way? how?*

R

rapiō, rapere, rapuī, raptum: *to snatch, to steal*
religiō, religōnis, f.: *religious scruple, superstition, cult*

relinquō, relinquere, relīquī, relictum: *to leave behind, to abandon*
reor, rērī, ratus sum: *think, deem, regard*
repetō, repetere, repetīvī or -iī, repetītum: *to repeat, to try again*
rēs, reī, f.: *thing, matter, object*
respondeō, respondēre, respondī, responsum: *to reply, to answer*
restō, -āre, restitī: *to hold firm, to resist, to be left*
rīdeō, rīdēre, rīsī, rīsum: *to laugh*
rogō, rogāre, rogāvī, rōgātum: *to ask, to beg, to request*

S

sabbata, -ōrum, n., pl.: *Sabbath*
Sabellus, -a, -um: *Sabellian, referring to an Italic tribe*
sacer, sacra, sacrum: *holy, sacred*
salsus, -a, -um: *facetious, humorous, witty*
salvus, -a, -um: *whole, safe and sound*
sānus, -a, -um: *sane, healthy*
sapiō, sapere, sapīvī or -iī: *to know, to be wise*
sciō, scīre, scīvī, scītum: *to know*
scrībō, ere, scrīpsī, scrīptum: *to write*
sēcrētō: adv., *in secret, secretly*
secundus, -a, -um: *following, favorable, supporting*
sed: conj., *but*
sequor, sequī, secūtus sum: *to follow*
servō, servāre, servāvī, servātum: *to save, to protect*
servus, -ī, m.: *slave, servant*
sī: conj., *if, whether*
sīc: adv., *so, as*
sīcut: conj., *just as, as*
simul: adv., *at the same time, at once*
sine: prep. w. abl., *without*
sōdēs: contracted form of **si audēs,** *if you will, please*
sōl, sōlis, m.: *sun, day*

stō, stāre, stetī, statum: *to stand, to take sides, to take part*
suāviter: adv., *smoothly*
sub: prep. w. abl., *under, beneath*
subeō, -īre, -īvī or -iī, -itum: *to enter, to approach, to undergo, to endure*
sūdor, sūdōris, m.: *sweat, hard work*
sum, esse, fuī, futūrus: *to be*
summoveō (= submoveō), summovēre, summōvī, summōtum: *to move up, to advance, to clear (i.e. the court), to drive away, to banish*
surgō, surgere, surrexī, surrectum: *to get up, to spring up, to rise*
suus, -a, -um: *one's own*

T

tacitus, -a, -um: *silent*
tālus, -ī, m.: *ankle, anklebone, heel*
tam: correlative adv., *so*
tantum: adv., *only*
tantummodo: adv., *only*
tardus, -a, -um: *slow, sluggish, lazy*
tēcum: cum + tē, see **tu**
tempus, temporis, n.: *time*
tendō, tendere, tetendī, tentum: *to stretch, to head for, to march*
tēne: tē + -ne, see **tu**
teneō, ēre, tenuī, tentum: *to hold, to hang on*
Tiberis, -is, m.: *Tiber, the river that runs through Rome*
totus, -a, -um: *whole, entire*
trādō, trādere, trādidī, trāditum: *to hand over, to hand down*
trans: prep. w. acc., *across, over, beyond*
trīcēsimus, -a, -um: *thirtieth*
tristis, -e: *sad, melancholy*
trivium, -ī, n.: *crossroads, intersection, public street*
tū: pers. pron., *you* (sing.)
tunc: adv., *then*

turpis, -e: *shameful, wretched*
tussis, -is, f.: *cough*
tuus, -a, -um: *your* (sing.)

U

ullus, -a, -um: *any*
unde: adv., *whence, where from*
undique: adv., *on all sides*
ūnus, -a, -um: see **ūnusquisque**; *one, only one*
ūnusquisque: *every single one*
urbs, urbis, f.: *city, Rome*
urna, -ae, f.: *jar, urn*
ūrō, ūrere, ussī, ustum: *to burn, to parch, to scorch*
usque: adv., *up till, as far as*
ut: conj., *as*
ūtor, ūtī, ūsus sum: *use, enjoy, practice* (+ abl.)
utrimque: adv., *from or on both sides, on either side*

V

vadōr, -ārī, vadātus sum: *to put someone under bail*
valeō, ēre, valuī: *to be able*
Varius -ī, m.: *Varius, a friend of Horace*
vellō, -ere, vellī or **vulsī, vulsum:** *to pluck, to pull, to tear at, to tweak*
venēnum, -ī, n.: *poison, drug*
veniō, venīre, vēnī, ventum: *to come, to arrive*
vērō: adv., *surely, in truth, in fact, however*
versus, -ūs, m.: *verse, line of poetry*
Vesta, -ae, f.: *Vesta, goddess of the hearth*
via, -ae, f.: *road, way*
victor, victōris, m.: *victor, conqueror, winner*
vīcus, -ī, m.: *village, hamlet, neighborhood*
videō, vidēre, vīdī, vīsum: *to see*

vīn: contracted form of **vīs ne**, see **volō**
vincō, vincere, vīcī, victum: *to conquer, to defeat*
virtūs, virtūtis, f.: *virtue, strength, gallantry, excellence, worth, moral perfection*
Viscus, -ī, m.: *Viscus, a friend of Horace*
vīsō, vīsere, vīsī, vīsum: *to look at attentively, to regard*
vīta, -ae, f.: *life*
vītō, -āre, -āvī, -ātum: *to avoid, to evade*
vīvō, vīvere, vixī, victum: *to live*
vix: *hardly*
volō, velle, voluī: *to wish*
vox, vōcis, f.: *voice, cry*

ORAL PROFICIENCY: MUSIC

Rome's Golden Poets
St. Louis Chamber Chorus

With its chronological, cultural, and ethnic diversity of composers, this recording testifies to the timeless power of the Golden Age of poetry. Selections from Catullus, Vergil, and Horace are performed by the St. Louis Chamber Chorus under the direction of Philip Barnes.

Limited edition CD
ISBN 0-86516-474-6

Latin Music Through the Ages
Cynthia Kaldis

Cassette features choral performance of seventeen Latin songs.

ISBN 0-86516-249-2

Book with lyrics, English translations, vocabulary; composer biographies, background on social/historical significance of each song, and illustrations.

ISBN 0-86516-242-5

Latine Cantemus: Cantica Popularia Latine Reddita
Translated and illustrated
by Franz Schlosser

This illustrated edition features sixty new Latin translations of popular songs, including nursery rhymes, chanties, folk songs, spirituals, and Christmas carols. Also included are three appendices of traditional Latin favorites, Christmas songs, and well-known Gregorian chants.

ISBN 0-86516-315-4

Schola Cantans
Composed by Jan Novák
Sung by Voces Latinae

A cassette with musical arrangement of **Catullus** (34) *Dianae Sumus in Fide;* **Catullus** (5) *Vivamus Mea Lesbia;* **Catullus** (61) *Collis O Heliconii;* **Horace** (Carm. 1, 22) *Integer Vitae;* **Horace** (Carm. 1,2) *Iam Satis Terris;* **Horace** (epod. 15) *Nox Erat;* **(Anonym.)** *Gaudeamus Igitur;* **Anth. Lat.** (388) *Nautarum Carmen;* **Caesar** (BG 1, 1–3) *Gallia Est Omnis Divisa;* **Carmina Burana** (142) *Tempus Adest Floridum;* **Carmina Burana** (85) *Veris Dulcis in Tempore;* **Martial** (10, 62) *Ludi Magister;* **Phaedrus** (1,13) *Vulpis et Corvus.*

Cassette is accompanied by a libretto with original Latin text and English translation on facing pages. Music score also available.

Cassette
19 pp. (1998), ISBN 0-86516-357-X

Music Score
46 pp. (1998), ISBN 0-86516-358-8

Cassette and Music Score Set
(1998), ISBN 0-86516-404-5

Vergil's *Dido & Mimus Magicus*
Composed by Jan Novák
Conducted by Rafael Kubelik
Performed by the Symphony Orchestra of the *Bayerischer Rundfunk* (Germany)
Original record published by audite Schallplatten, Germany

Limited Edition CD (1997)
40-page libretto in Latin, English, and German
ISBN 0-86516-346-4

BOLCHAZY-CARDUCCI Publishers, Inc. ✦ http://www.bolchazy.com

REFERENCES & RESOURCES

Gildersleeve's Latin Grammar
B. L. Gildersleeve and G. Lodge

The classic Latin grammar favored by many students and teachers with two new addtions
+ Foreword
Ward W. Briggs, Jr.
+ Comprehensive bibliography
William E. Wycislo

The 45-page bibliography that accompanies our new reprint is designed primarily but not exclusively for an American audience, comprising scholarship produced on Latin grammar in English during this century.

613 pp. (1895, Third ed., Reprint with additions 1997)
Paperback, ISBN 0-86516-353-7

A New Latin Syntax
E. C. Woodcock

xxiv + 267 pp. (1959, Reprint 1987)
Paperback, ISBN 0-86516-126-7

Smith's English-Latin Dictionary
William Smith and Theophilus D. Hall

Smith's English-Latin Dictionary is an invaluable resource for students and teachers who are composing Latin verse and prose. Each entry is composed of an English word, its corresponding Latin equivalents, and examples drawn from a full range of classical writers. The index of proper names contains the Latin forms of names of thousands of persons, places, and geographical features from Greco-Roman history and mythology, as well as the Judeo-Christian Bible.

(2000) Paperback, ISBN 0-86516-491-6
Hardbound, ISBN 0-86516-492-4

Graphic Latin Grammar
James P. Humphreys

An invaluable quick reference—no need for busy students to keep flipping to the back of the book to look up forms, or search chapters for a review of syntax. These card contain paradigms of regular, irregular, and deponent verbs, nouns, adjectives, pronouns, and numerals; plus charts of prepositions and adverbs; and a guide to syntax of cases and syntax of nouns—all in an easily readable and highly durable format.

(1961, Reprint 1995)
Four 3-hole-punched reference cards, Laminated, ISBN 0-86516-111-1

New Latin Composition
Charles E. Bennett

ix + 292 pp. (1912, Reprint 1996)
Paperback, ISBN 0-86516-345-6

Latin Prose Composition and Key to Latin Prose Composition
M. A. North and A. E. Hillard

Latin Prose Composition is aimed at helping students to enhance their command of Latin grammar and vocabulary. The exercises have been structured in a manner that gradually enables students to build their Latin prose skills. *Key to Latin Prose Composition* is an invaluable teacher's manual.

Latin Prose Composition
xix + 300 pp. (Reprint 1995)
Paperback, ISBN 0-86516-308-1

Key to Latin Prose Composition
108 pp. (Reprint 1995)
Paperback, ISBN 0-86516-307-3

BOLCHAZY-CARDUCCI Publishers, Inc. ✦ http://www.bolchazy.com

Why Horace?

A Collection of Interpretations
by William S. Anderson

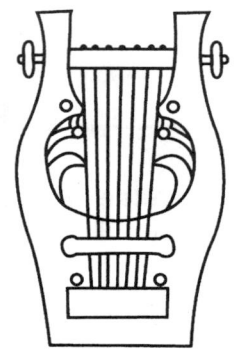

Table of Contents

Introduction

Horace: Odes I
Arthur J. Pomeroy, A Man at a Spring: Horace, *Odes* 1.1
D. W. Thomson Vessey, Pyrrha's Grotto and the Farewell to Love: A Study of Horace *Odes* 1.5
Niall Rudd, Patterns in Horatian Lyric
William S. Anderson, Horace's Different Recommenders of *Carpe Diem* in C. 1.4, 7, 9, 11
Charles Segal, Felices ter et amplius: Horace, *Odes*, I. 13
Gregson Davis, *Carmina/Iambi*: The Literary-Generic Dimension of Horace's *Integer Vitae* (C. 1, 22)
Ronnie Ancona, The Subterfuge of Reason: Horace, *Odes* 1.23 and the Construction of Male Desire
H. Akbar Khan, Horace's Ode to Virgil on the Death of Quintilius: 1.24
William S. Anderson, The Secret of Lydia's Aging: Horace, *Odes* 1.25
W. R. Johnson, A Quean, a Great Queen? Cleopatra and the Politics of Misrepresentation
William Fitzgerald, Horace, Pleasure and the Text

Horace: Odes II
A. J. Woodman, Horace, *Odes*, II, 3
John L. Moles, Politics, Philosophy, and Friendship in Horace: *Odes* 2,7
Christopher J. Reagan, Horace, *Carmen* 2.10: The Use of Oxymoron as a Thematic Statement
William S. Anderson, The Occasion of Horace's *Carm.* 2.14

Horace: Odes III
Charles Witke, Horace and the Roman Odes
Michael C. J. Putnam, Horace *Odes* 3.9: The Dialectics of Desire
William Fitzgerald, Horace, Pleasure and the Text (Part 2)
Tony Woodman, EXEGI MONVMENTVM: Horace, *Odes* 3.30

Horace: Odes IV
E. A. Fredricksmeyer, Horace, *Odes* 4.7: "The Most Beautiful Poem in Ancient Literature"?

Horace: Satire I.9
William S. Anderson, Horace, The Unwilling Warrior: *Satire* I.9

Bibliography on Horace

xvi + 264 pp. (1999), *Paperback:* ISBN 0-86516-417-7
xvi + 264 pp. (1999), *Hardbound:* ISBN 0-86516-434-7

BOLCHAZY-CARDUCCI Publishers, Inc. ✦ http://www.bolchazy.com